CHOPIN FREDERIC

SHEET MUSIC SOLO PIANO MISCELLANEOUS

ISBN: 978-1-80221-021-7

CONTENT

- CITATIONS OF THE LIFE AND WORK — PAGE 4
- TEMATIX INDEX — PAGE 5
- VARIATIONS BRILLANTES IN B FLAT MAJOR, OP.12 — PAGE 6
- BOLERO IN A MINOR, OP.19 — PAGE 17
- TARANTELLE IN A FLAT MAJOR, OP.43 — PAGE 28
- ALLEGRO DE CONCERT IN A MAJOR, OP.46 — PAGE 38
- FANTASIE IN F MINOR, OP.49 — PAGE 53
- BERCEUSE IN D FLAT MAJOR, OP.57 — PAGE 72
- BARCAROLLE IN F SHARP MAJOR, OP.60 — PAGE 79
- MARCHE FUNEBRE IN C MINOR, OP.72, NO.2 — PAGE 87
- 3 ECOSSAISES, OP.72, NO.3 — PAGE 91
- VARIATIONS ON "DER SCHWEIZERBUB", B.14 — PAGE 96

Citations of the life and works in the book

Frédéric Chopin was born on March 1, 1810, in Żelazowa Wola, near Warsaw, Poland. He was the son of a French teacher and a Polish mother and showed an extraordinary talent for the piano at a young age. He studied with the famous Polish pianist and composer Józef Elsner and began composing from a young age.

Chopin moved to Paris at the age of 21 and spent much of his life there. He became a prominent figure in Parisian cultural life, frequenting literary and artistic salons and becoming famous as a piano teacher. His music was admired by both critics and audiences, and he was considered one of the greatest composers of his time.

However, his life was marked by illness, particularly tuberculosis which afflicted him for many years and eventually led to his death in 1849, at the age of only 39. His romantic relationship with the French writer George Sand was equally tumultuous and ended dramatically shortly before his death.

Despite his short life, Chopin left a significant musical legacy. His piano music is known for its beauty, virtuosity, and poetic sensitivity, and has influenced numerous composers who followed him. Chopin was one of the first composers to write almost exclusively for solo piano and developed a distinctive musical style that deeply marked romantic music.

Frédéric Chopin is widely recognized as one of the greatest composers of the Romantic era, and his output is mainly composed of solo piano pieces such as ballades, études, impromptus, mazurkas, nocturnes, polonaises, preludes, rondos, scherzos, sonatas, and waltzes. His virtuosic and expressive compositions for the piano remain staples of the repertoire to this day.

Aside from these works, Chopin also wrote several other pieces, primarily for solo piano but also for other instruments. While some of these compositions are well-known, some included in this book, such as the **Barcarolle in F-sharp, the Fantaisie in F minor, the Berceuse in D-flat,** and a selection of 19 Polish songs, many others remained relatively unknown until after his death. In fact, Chopin had specifically requested that all of his unpublished manuscripts be destroyed, which means that some of these compositions were only discovered and published posthumously.

Although these miscellaneous works are not as frequently performed in the concert repertoire, they are still an integral part of Chopin's oeuvre and have been recorded numerous times. They offer a glimpse into the lesser-known aspects of Chopin's musical creativity and add depth to our understanding of this great composer's legacy.

Thematic Index.

VARIATIONS BRILLANTES IN B FLAT MAJOR, OP.12

Variations brillantes.
Op. 12.
(Sur le Rondeau favori: „Je vends des Scapulaires" de Ludovic.)

Introduction.
Allegro maestoso. ($\quarter = 118.$)

Thème.
Allegro moderato.

BOLERO IN A MINOR, OP.19

Bolero.
Op.19.

Introduzione.
Molto allegro. (♩ = 88.)

TARANTELLE IN A FLAT MAJOR, OP.43

Tarentelle.

F. CHOPIN. Op. 43.

ALLEGRO DE CONCERT IN A MAJOR, OP.46

Allegro de Concert.
Op.46.

FANTASIE IN F MINOR, OP.49

FANTAISIE.

à Mme la Princesse CATH. de SOUZZO.

F. CHOPIN. Op. 49.

Tempo di marcia.

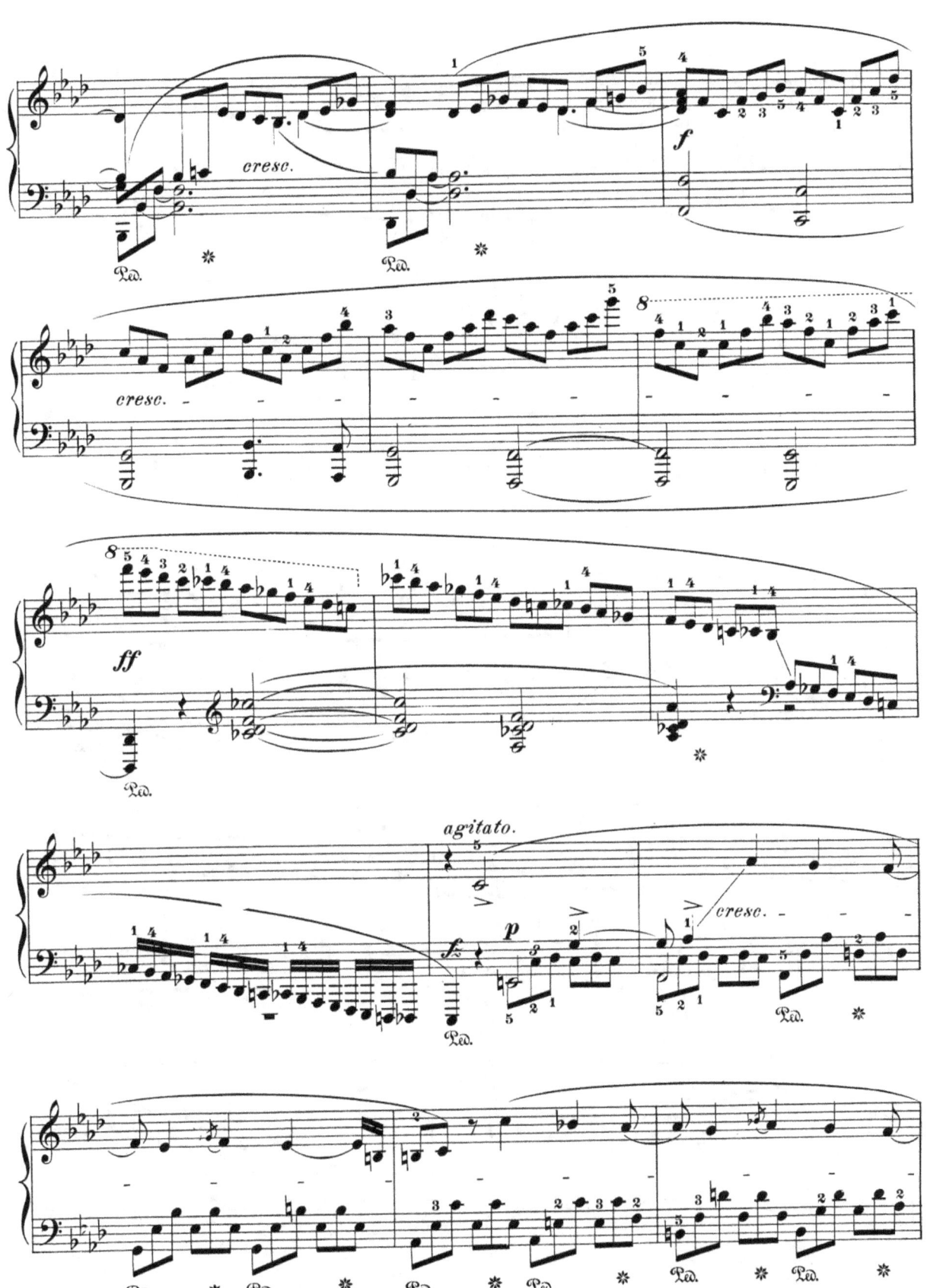

60

BERCEUSE IN D FLAT MAJOR, OP.57

A Mlle Elise Gavard.

Berceuse.

F. Chopin, Op. 57.

Andante.

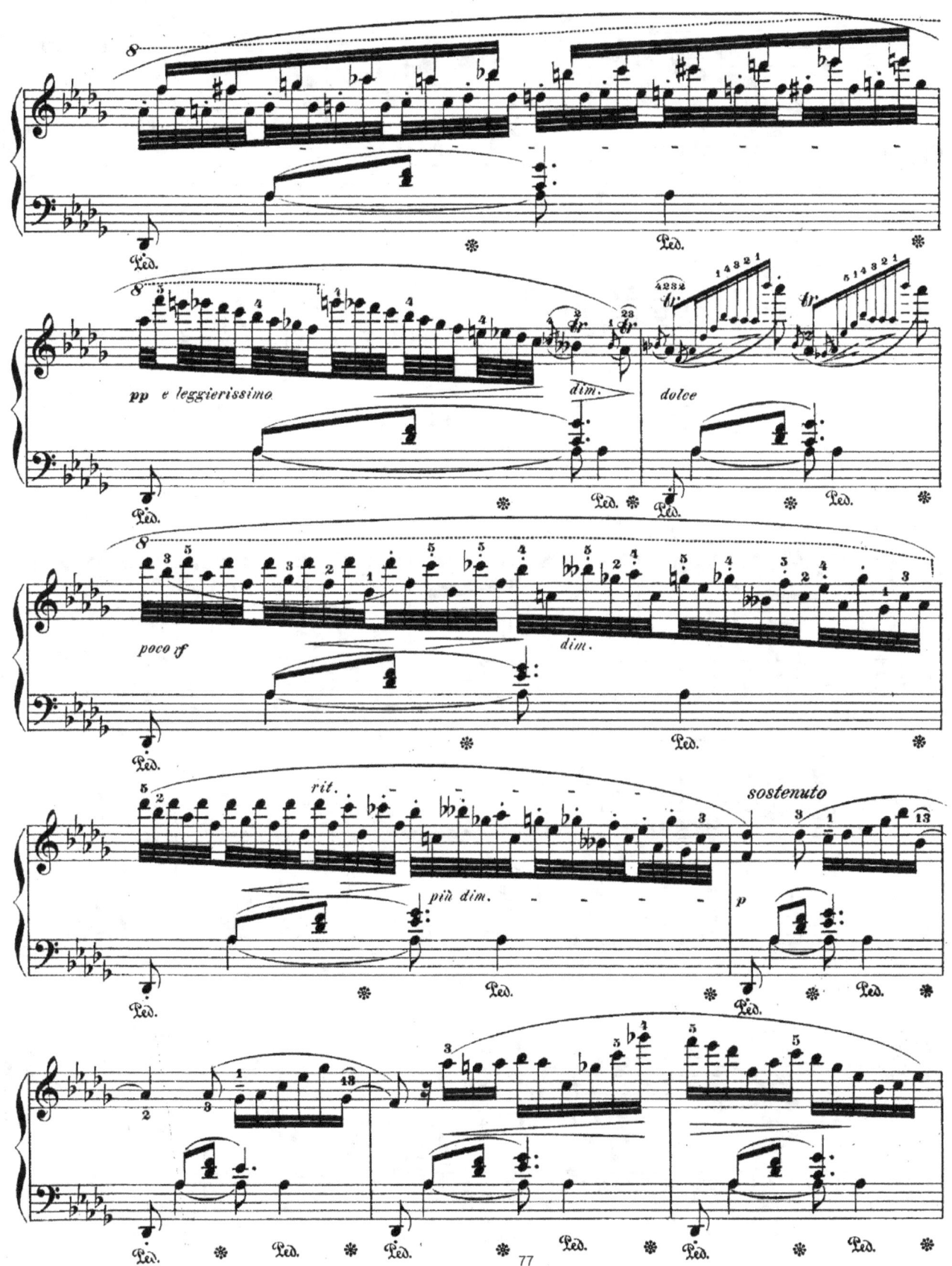

BARCAROLLE IN F SHARP MAJOR, OP.60

Barcarolle.
Op. 60.

MARCHE FUNEBRE IN C MINOR, OP.72, NO.2

Marche funèbre.

(Posthumous.)

F. CHOPIN. Op. 72, No 2.
(1829.)

Tempo di Marcia. (♩= 84.)

3 ECOSSAISES, OP.72, NO.3

Trois Ecossaises.
(Posthumous.)

F. CHOPIN. Op. 72, No 3.
(1880.)

F. CHOPIN. Op. 72, N⁰ 4.

F. CHOPIN. Op.72, No 5.

VARIATIONS ON "DER SCHWEIZERBUB", B.14

Variations.
(Sur un Air national-allemand.)
Oeuvre posthume.

Introduzione.
A capriccio.

Var. 4.
Meno mosso.

attacca:

www.ingramcontent.com/pod-product-compliance
Lightning Source LLC
Chambersburg PA
CBHW081622100526
44590CB00021B/3555